A Century of
Westward Expansion

edited by
JoAnne Weisman Deitch

Panning for gold. (Mediasource, Historical Picture Service, Inc.)

Discovery Enterprises, Ltd.
Carlisle, Massachusetts

First Edition © Discovery Enterprises, Ltd., Carlisle, MA 2000

ISBN 1-57960-064-6

Library of Congress Catalog Card Number 00-103463

10 9 8 7 6 5 4 3 2 1

Printed in the United States of America

Subject Reference Guide:

Title: *A Century of Westward Expansion*
Series*: Researching American History*
edited by JoAnne Weisman Deitch

Nonfiction
Analyzing documents re: Westward Expansion 1800-1900;
The Lewis and Clark Expedition
Zebulon Pike
Trappers and Traders
Trails West
The Gold Rush
The Pony Express
Building the Transcontinental Railroad

Credits:

Cover art: Arkansas storefronts as covered wagon train arrives
(Courtesy of Mediasource, Historical Picture Service, Inc.)

All other graphics are cited where they appear in the text.

Special Thanks:

To the editors of the following books in the *Perspectives on History Series* for the use of their research and introductory materials:

Cheryl Edwards - *Westward Expansion: Exploration and Settlement*

Phyllis R. Emert - *All That Glitters: Men and Women of the Gold and Silver Rushes*

Jeanne Munn Bracken - *Iron Horses across America: The Transcontinental Railroad*

Katharine N. Emsden - *Voices from the West: Life along the Trail*

Contents

About the Series

Researching American History is a series of books which introduces various topics and periods in our nation's history through the study of primary source documents.

Reading the Historical Documents

On the following pages you'll find words written by people during or soon after the time of the events. This is firsthand information about what life was like back then. Illustrations are also created to record history. These historical documents are called **primary source materials**.

At first, some things written in earlier times may seem hard to understand. Language changes over the years, and the objects and activities described might be unfamiliar. Also, spellings were sometimes different. Below is a model which describes how we help with these challenges.

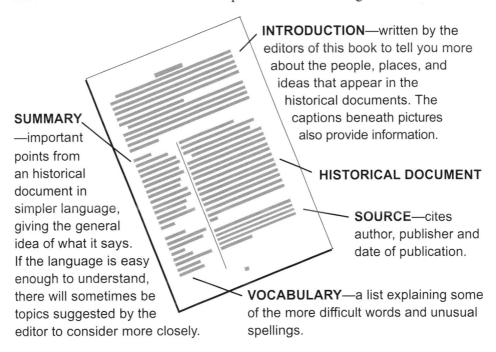

INTRODUCTION—written by the editors of this book to tell you more about the people, places, and ideas that appear in the historical documents. The captions beneath pictures also provide information.

SUMMARY—important points from an historical document in simpler language, giving the general idea of what it says. If the language is easy enough to understand, there will sometimes be topics suggested by the editor to consider more closely.

HISTORICAL DOCUMENT

SOURCE—cites author, publisher and date of publication.

VOCABULARY—a list explaining some of the more difficult words and unusual spellings.

In these historical documents, you may see three periods (...) called an ellipsis. It means that the editor has left out some words or sentences. You may see some words in brackets, such as [and]. These are words the editor has added to make the meaning clearer. When you use a document in a paper you're writing, you should include any ellipses and brackets it contains, just as you see them here. Be sure to give complete information about the author, title, and publisher of anything that was written by someone other than you.

Introduction:
A Century of Westward Expansion

by

JoAnne Weisman Deitch

Not long after the east coast colonies were bustling centers of activity in the 1700s, people began to think about going West. By the time the American Revolution ended in 1783, the wilderness stretching beyond the Ohio Country—the uncharted Louisiana Province, belonging to Spain—seemed very tempting to Americans desiring more land, good hunting, and the opportunity for trapping and trading furs.

Early frontiersmen like Daniel Boone and Davy Crockett helped to open access to the Ohio Country by clearing trails and passes through the mountains. Although these crude roads provided routes to the West, they were tedious to travel. Travelers were often met with resistance from native tribes who had lived there for centuries, and the rugged terrain posed numerous challenges to the inexperienced pioneers.

Americans soon looked to waterways like the Mississippi and Ohio Rivers, which provided a faster and less expensive solution. Traders could ship their merchandise right to the Spanish-controlled Port of New Orleans. When Spain gave the Louisiana Province to France, out of gratitude for their help in defeating the British in the Revolutionary War, President Thomas Jefferson was concerned that Americans might lose their access to the port. Wanting to avoid war with another European country, in 1803, Jefferson purchased the Louisiana Province from France for $15 million, doubling the size of the United States. This purchase was to begin one hundred years of westward expansion, settlement, and growth in communications and transportation for the new nation, as well as the displacement and devastation of the Native American tribal nations they encountered along the way.

The natural resources and economic opportunities to be had in the West would change the face of America forever. In the century to follow, gold would be discovered, the Pony Express established, a transcontinental railroad built, telegraph wires stretched across the land, homesteaders settling the plains, trappers and traders establishing prosperous trade routes, and religious groups like the Mormons seeking their own piece of the promised land.

By the end of the 19th century, the United States had taken over much of what was previously Indian territory to the West and a large portion of Mexico to the Southwest, making the country the most powerful and prosperous nation in North America and the world.

Lewis and Clark

Shortly after the Purchase of Louisiana, President Jefferson commissioned Meriwether Lewis and William Clark to explore the Louisiana Territory, to study and document its natural resources, establish trade with the Indians, and discover a passage to the Pacific Ocean.

Jefferson's Letter to Lewis and Clark

An excerpt from his letter to them follows, with original misspellings, sentence structure, and punctuation intact.

Summary:

The object of the mission is to explore the Missouri River, its streams, and its connection to the Pacific Ocean, to determine the most direct way across the continent.

Map all positions and special characteristics and locations, using a compass. The interesting points on the land should be noted, too.

The observations should be accurate and easy for others to understand. Latitudes and longitudes of all points should be recorded.

Vocabulary:

comprehend = understand

durable = lasting

latitude = distance north or south of equator

longitude = east/west of the prime meridian

portage = land where boats must be carried

…the object of your mission is to explore the Missouri river, & such principal stream of it, as, by it's course & communication with the water of the Pacific Ocean may offer the most direct & practicable water communication across the continent, for the purposes of commerce.

Beginning at the mouth of the Missouri, you will take observations of latitude and longitude at all remarkable points on the river, & especially at the mouths of rivers, at rapids, at marks & characters of a durable kind, as that they may with certainty be recognized hereafter. The courses of the river between these points of observations may be supplied by the compass, the log-line & by time, corrected by the observations themselves. The variations of the compass too, in different places should be noticed.

The interesting points of the portage between the heads of the Missouri & the water offering the best communication with the Pacific Ocean should be fixed by observation & the course of that water to the ocean, in the same manner as that of the Missouri.

Your observations are to be taken with great pains & accuracy, to be entered distinctly, & intelligibly for others as well as yourself, to comprehend all the elements necessary, with the aid of the usual tables to fix the latitude & longitude of the places at which they were taken,

& are to be rendered to the war office, for the purpose of having the calculations made concurrently by proper persons within the U.S. Several copies of these as well as of your other notes, should be made at leisure times & put into the care of the most trustworthy of your attendants, to guard by multiplying them against the accidental losses to which they will be exposed. A further guard would be that one of these copies be written on the paper of the birch, as less liable to injury from damp than common paper.

The commerce which may be carried on with the people inhabiting the line you will pursue, renders a knolege of these people important. You will therefore endeavor to make yourself — acquainted, as far as a diligent pursuit of your journey shall admit.

with the names of the nations & their numbers; the extent & limits of their possessions; their relations with other tribes or nations: their language, traditions, monuments; their ordinary occupations in agriculture, fishing, hunting,

war, arts, & the implements for these; their food, clothing, & domestic accommodations; the diseases prevalent among them, & the remedies they use;

moral and physical circumstance which distinguish them from the tribes they know; peculiarities in their laws, customs & dispositions; and articles of commerce they may need or furnish & to what extent.

. . . .

Other objects worthy of notice will be the soil & face of the country, its growth & vegetable productions; especially those not of the U.S.

animals of the country generally, & especially those not known in the U.S.

The remains & accounts of any which may be deemed rare or extinct;

Summary:
The notes should be given to the war office. Several copies should be made when there's time. Make a copy on birch bark so the dampness doesn't ruin it.

Make notes on the business and trade practices of those you meet.

Record the names of the tribes, their possessions, their relationships to other tribes, their languages, customs, traditions, occupations, arts, living conditions, etc. Also record the geography, wildlife, vegetation, especially not known in the U.S.

Vocabulary:
circumstance = determining factor
commerce = business
concurrently = happening at the same time
deemed = thought to be
dispositions = temperament
endeavor = an earnest attempt
extinct = no longer existing
implements = tools
knolege = knowledge
prevalent = generally accepted

Summary:

Record the minerals, the climate, the seasons for plant life, migration of animals, etc.

Treat the natives well and assure them you are there in peace. Discuss trading with them. See what they're interested in. If a few chiefs want to visit with us, we will arrange a visit. If some of their young people would like to be educated by us, we will arrange it. That would make your situation more secure. Make sure you have some medicine with you.

Vocabulary:

allay = calm, pacify
conciliatory = placating, soothing manner
confer = consult
emporiums = marketplaces
intercourse = interchange, communication

the mineral productions of every kind; but more particularly metals, limestone, pit coal & salt-petre; salines & mineral waters, noting the temperature of the last & such circumstances as may indicate their character; volcanic appearances;

climate as characterized by the thermometer, by the proportion of rainy, cloudy & clear days, by lightening, hail, snow, ice, by the access & recess of frost, by the winds, prevailing at different seasons, the dates at which particular plants put forth or lose their flowers, or leaf, times of appearance of particular birds, reptiles or insects.

. . . .

In all your intercourse with the natives treat them in the most friendly & conciliatory manner which their own conduct will admit; allay all jealousies as to the object of your journey, satisfy them of it's innocence, make them acquainted with the position, extent, character, peaceable & commercial dispositions of the U.S., of our wish to be neighborly, friendly & useful to them, & of our dispositions to a commercial intercourse with them; confer with them on the points most convenient as mutual emporiums, & the articles of most desirable interchange for them & us. If a few of their influential chiefs, within practicable distance, wish to visit us, arrange such a visit with them, and furnish them with authority to call on our officers, on their entering the U.S. to have them conveyed to this place at the public expense. If any of them should wish to have some of their young people brought up with us, & taught such arts as may be useful to them, we will receive, instruct & take care of them. Such a mission, whether of influential chiefs, or of young people, would give some security to your own party. Carry with you some matter of the kine-pox, inform those of them with whom you may be of it's efficacy as a preservative from the small-pox; and instruct & encourage them in the use of it....

. . . .

Should you reach the Pacific Ocean inform yourself of the circumstances which may decide whether the furs of those parts may not be collected as advantageously at the head of the Missouri (convenient as is supposed to the waters of the Colorado & Oregon or Columbia) as at Nootka Sound or any other point of that coast; & that trade be consequently conducted through the Missouri & U.S. more beneficially than by the circumnavigation now practised.

On your arrival on that coast endeavor to learn if there be any port within your reach frequented by the sea-vessels of any nation, and to send two of your trusted people back by sea, ..., with a copy of your notes. And should you be of the opinion that the return of your party by the way they went will be eminently dangerous, then ship the whole, & return by sea by way of Cape Horn or the Cape of Good Hope, as you shall be able. As you will be without money, clothes or provisions, you must endeavor to use the credit of the U.S. to obtain them; for which purpose open letters of credit shall be furnished you authorizing you to draw on the Executive of the U.S. or nay of its officers in any part of the world, in which drafts can be disposed of, and to apply with our recommendations to the consuls, agents, merchants or citizens of any nation with which we have intercourse, assuring them in our name that any aids they may furnish you, shall be honorably repaid and on demand....

Source: Thomas Jefferson, *Thomas Jefferson Writings.* The Library of America, pp. 1127, 1129-31.

Summary:
The medicine should be effective against smallpox. Encourage them to use it.

If you reach the Pacific Ocean, see if it's a good place to trap for furs.

When you arrive at the coast, try to learn if there are busy seaports. If so, send two of your most trusted people back here with a copy of your notes. If you think it will be dangerous for your whole group to return the way you went, then all of you should get on a ship to come back here. You don't have money, but tell the people involved that the government will pay them back for everything you need.

Vocabulary:
circumnavigation = sailing completely around
efficacy = effectiveness
eminently = prominently, outstandingly
frequented = visited often

The Journals of Lewis and Clark

The following excerpts contain information on exploration of the Missouri and Columbia Rivers, flora and fauna, Native Americans, life on the expedition, and a description of the discovery of an intercontinental route to the Pacific Ocean.

Summary:

We found the remains of buffaloes along the shore. They had fallen through the ice and drowned, and washed up on shore when the ice melted. We also saw tracks of the white bears. The Indians tell us that this is a frightening animal. They seldom dare to hunt it unless there are six, eight, or ten men along. They paint themselves and perform other superstitious rights when they go to shoot a bear.

Vocabulary:

abundant = plentiful
carcases = dead bodies
formidable = awe-inspiring

[Lewis]   Saturday April 13th

…we found a number of carcases of the Buffaloe lying along shore, which had been drowned by falling through the ice in winter and lodged on shore by the high water when the river broke up about the first of this month. we saw also many tracks of the white bear of enormous size, along the river shore and about the carcases of the Buffaloe, on which I presume they feed. we have not yet seen one of these animals, tho' their tracks are so abundant and recent. the men as well as ourselves are anxious to meet with some of these bear. the Indians give a very formidable account of the strenth and ferocity of this anamal, which they never dare to attack but in parties of six eight or ten persons; and are even then frequently defeated with the loss of one or more of their party. the savages attack this animal with their bows and arrows and the indifferent guns with which the traders furnish them, with these they shoot with such uncertainty and at so short a distance, that (unless shot thro' head or heart wound not mortal) they frequently mis their aim & fall a sacrefice to the bear. this anamall is said more frequently to attack a man on meeting with him, than to flee from him. When the Indians are about to go in quest of the white bear, previous to their departure, they paint themselves and perform all those supersticious rights commonly observed when they are about to make war uppon a neighbouring nation. Observed more bald eagles on this part of the Missouri than we have previously seen. saw the small hawk, frequently called the sparrow hawk, which is common to most parts of the U. States. great quantities of gees are seen feeding in the praries. saw a large flock of white brant or gees with black wings pass up the river; there were a number of gray brant with them.

Summary:
We've seen a lot of bald eagles, sparrow hawks, geese, white, and gray brant.

Lewis' journal page with a drawing of a bird.

[Clark]   October 28th Monday 1805

A cool windey morning we loaded our canoes and Set out at 9 oclock, a.m. as we were about to set out 3 canoes from above and 2 from below came to view us in one of those canoes I observed an Indian with round hat Jacket & wore his hair cued we proceeded on at four miles we landed at a Village of 8 houses on the Stard. Side under some rugid rocks, I entered one of the houses in which I saw a British musket, a cutlash and Several brass Tea kitties

Summary:
  In one of the houses I saw a gun, a sword, several brass tea kettles.

Vocabulary:
rugid = rugged

Summary:

We saw them boiling fish in baskets with stones. We bought some dogs, berries, and bread. It got very windy, but that didn't stop the Indians from using their canoes. The canoes are built of white cedar or pine. They are tapered on the ends. The heads of animals are carved on the bow. It was rainy and windy all evening. We camped in wet sand.

Vocabulary:

buries = berries
cutlash = a sword
fiew = few
tapers = narrows

Vocabulary:

brackfast = breakfast
induced = persuaded
Sumptious = sumptuous, lavish

of which they appeared verry fond Saw them boiling fish in baskets with Stones, here we purchased five Small Dogs, Some dried buries, & white bread made of roots, the wind rose and we were obliged to lie by all day at I mile below on the Lard Side. we had not been long on Shore before a Canoe came up with a man woman & 2 children, who had a fiew roots to Sell, Soon after many others joined them from above, The wind which is the cause of our delay, does not retard the motions of those people at all, as their canoes are calculated to ride the highest waves, they are built of white cedar or Pine verry light wide in the middle and tapers at each end, with aperns, and heads of animals carved on the bow, which is generally raised. wind blew hard accompanied with rain all the evening, our Situation not a verry good one for an encampment, but such as it is we are obliged to put up with, the harbor Is a Safe one, we encamped on the Sand, wet and disagreeable.

November the 19th 1805.

I arose early this morning from under a Wet blanket caused by a Shower of rain which fell in the latter part of the last night, and Sent two men on a head with directions to proceed on near the Sea Coast and Kill Something for brackfast and that I should follow my self in about half an hour. after drying our blankets a little I set out with a view to proceed near the Coast the direction of which induced me to conclude that at the distance of 8 or 10 miles, the Bay was at no great distance across. I overtook the hunters at about 3 miles, they had killed a Small Deer on which we brackfast[ed], it Comen[c]ed raining and continued moderately until 11 oclock A M. after taking a Sumptious brackfast of Venison which was roasted on Stiks exposed to the fire, I proceeded on through ruged Country of high hills and Steep hollers to the commencement of a Sandy coast which extended to a point of high land distant near 20 miles. this point I have taken the Liberty of Calling after my particular friend Lewis. at the commencement of this Sand beech the high lands leave the Sea Coast in a Direction to Chinnook river, and does not touch the Sea Coast again below point Lewis leaveing a low pondey Countrey, maney places open with small ponds in which there is great numbr. of fowl I am informed that the Chinnook Nation inhabit this low country and live in large wood houses on a river which passes through this bottom Parrilal to the Sea coast and falls into the Bay I proceeded on the sandy coast and marked my name on a Small pine, the Day of the month & year, &c. and returned to the foot of the hill, I saw a Sturgeon which had been thrown on Shore and left by the tide 10 feet in length, and Several joints of the back bone of a Whale, which must have foundered on this part of the Coast. after Dineing on the remains of our Small Deer I proceeded to the bay distance about 2 miles, thence up to the mouth of Chinnook river 2 miles, crossed this little river in the Canoe we left at its mouth and Encamped on the upper Side in any open sandy bottom.

Source: Bernard DeVoto, ed., *The Journals of Lewis and Clark*. Boston: Houghton Mifflin Company, The Riverside Press Cambridge, 1953, pp. 94-5, 267-8, 286-99.

Summary:

It rained until 11 A.M. We had a big breakfast, then proceeded through rugged country to the coast, where there was a point I named after Lewis. There are many small ponds and fowl. The Chinook Nation lives here. They live in large wooden houses on a river. I marked my name and the date on a small tree and returned to the foot of the hill. I saw a huge fish and the backbone of a whale on the beach. I had dinner and went back to the encampment.

Vocabulary:

foundered = became disabled

13

Zebulon Pike

Shortly after Lewis and Clark's expedition was completed, General James Wilkinson, commander-in-chief of the U.S. Army, sent young Zebulon Pike westward, to explore the Arkansas and Red Rivers. It was a difficult journey and Pike and his group suffered greatly from the cold. In Colorado the men attempted unsuccessfully to cross the snow-covered mountain that to this day bears his name—Pike's Peak.

Pike Describes Several of the Tribes

In 1805, Zebulon Pike was dispatched to the Mississippi River to explore the region and to document Native American tribes there.

Summary:

The Minowa Kantongs are the only Sioux who use canoes. They have a very civilized culture: they build log huts, plant vegetables, hunt and fish, and have firearms.

He describes the Yanctongs and Titongs as being independent, having horses, and able to move great distances quickly.

Vocabulary:
subsistence = livelihood

The Minowa Kantongs are the only band of Sioux who use canoes, and by far the most civilized, they being the only ones who have ever built log huts, or cultivated any species of vegetables; and those only a very small quantity of corn and beans; for although I was with them in September or October, I never saw one kettle of either, always using the wild oats for bread. This production nature has furnished to all the most uncultivated nations of the N.W. continent, who may gather a sufficiency in autumn, which, when added to the productions of the chase and the net, ensures them a subsistence through all the seasons of the year. This band is entirely armed with fire arms, but is not considered by the other bands as any thing superior on that account, especially on the plains.

'Me Washpetong are a roving band; they leave the river St. Peters in the month of April, and do not return from the plains, until the middle of August.... The Yanctongs and Titongs are the most independent Indians in the world; they follow the buffalo as chance directs; clothing themselves with the skin, and making their lodges, bridles, and saddles of the same material, the flesh of the animal furnishing their food.

Possessing innumerable herds of horses, they are here this day, 500 miles off ten days hence, and find themselves equally at home in either place, moving with a rapidity scarcely to be imagined by the inhabitants of the civilized world.

. . . .

From my knowledge of the Sioux nation, I do not hesitate to pronounce them the most warlike and independent nation of Indians within the boundaries of the United States, their every passion being subservient to that of war; but at the same time, their traders feel themselves perfectly secure of any combination being made against them, but it is extremely necessary to be careful not to injure the honor or feelings of an individual, which is certainly the principal cause of the many broils which occur between them.... Their guttural pronunciation; high cheek bones; their visages, and distinct manners, together with their own traditions, supported by the testimony of neighboring nations, puts in my mind, beyond the shadow of a doubt that they have emigrated from the N.W. point of America, to which they had come across the narrow straights, which in that quarter divides the two continents; and are absolutely descendants of a Tartarean tribe.

. . . .

The Algonquin language is one of the most copious and sonorous languages of all the savage dialects in North America; and is spoken and understood by the various nations (except the Sioux) from the Gulf of St. Lawrence to Lake Winipie.

Source: Donald Jackson, ed., *The Journals of Zebulon Montgomery Pike with Letters and Related Documents*, Vol. 1. University of Oklahoma Press: Norman, 1966, pp. 213-5.

Summary:
They are warlike because of their customs and characteristics. He believes they migrated from the northwest part of the continent.
The Algonquins have a highly developed language.

Vocabulary:
copious = abundant
guttural = sound coming from the throat
sonorous = producing a full, rich sound
subservient = serving to promote some end
visages = faces or facial expressions

Traders and Trappers

Ads like the one above, drew hundreds of men to the West, with dreams of adventure, independence, and wealth. Because of the fur market for hats and trim for coats in Europe, and to a lesser extent in the East, men were willing to face harsh winters, Indian attacks, and possible starvation, to capture as many beaver pelts as possible—each with a market price of $6-$9.

The life of a trapper was a lonely life, although some of the men who chose this lifestyle took Indian brides along as guides, companions, and cooks. The men were roughly clad and groomed—often wearing buckskin—with scraggly beards, long hair, and always armed with several weapons.

Although much of their time was spent alone, hunting and trapping, once a year they joined other trappers and traders at the *rendezvous* (French for meeting place), where they would trade stories, pelts, and plenty of alcohol and tobacco for weapons, and other necessities. The events often lasted for as long as two weeks. Fur trader William Ashley organized the first rendezvous in 1825 and they were held every July until 1840.

Jim Beckwourth

Jim Beckwourth was a runaway slave, who became a scout and a trapper, and later became Chief of the Crow Indians. His discovery of a pass over the Sierra Nevada mountains led frontiersmen to the gold fields of California The pass was named for him and still bears his name.

Beckwourth's account of finding the pass

We proceeded in an easterly direction, and all busied themselves in searching for gold; but my errand was of a different character; I had come to discover what I suspected to be a pass.

It was the latter end of April when we entered upon an extensive valley at the northwest extremity of the Sierra range.... Swarms of wild geese and ducks were swimming on the surface of the cool crystal stream, which was the central fork of the Rio de las Plumas, or sailed the air in clouds over our heads. Deer and antelope filled the plains and their boldness was conclusive that the hunter's rifle was to them unknown. Nowhere visible were any traces of the white man's approach, and it is probable that our steps were the first that ever marked the spot. We struck across this beautiful valley to the waters of the Yuba, from thence to the waters of the Truchy.... This, I at once saw, would afford the best waggon-road into the American Valley approaching from the eastward, and I imparted my views to three of my companions in whose judgment I placed the most confidence. They thought highly of the discovery, and even proposed to associate with me in opening the road. We also found gold, but not in sufficient quantity to warrant our worldng it....

On my return to the American Valley, I made known my discovery to a Mr. Turner, proprietor of the American Ranch, who entered enthusiastically into my views; it was a thing, he said, he had never dreamed of before.

Source: James Beckwourth, *The Life and Adventures of James Beckwourth, Mountaineer, Scout, Pioneer and Chief of the Crow Nation of Indians.* Written from his own dictation by T D Bonner (London, 1892), pp. 424-6.

Summary:

We continued easterly. The men were searching for gold, but my goal was to find a pass through the mountains.

At the end of April we came to the northwest part of the Sierra Range. We saw abundant wildlife, but no trace of white men. I spotted a good wagon road to the American Valley, approaching from the East. I asked three of my companions what they thought, and they agreed with me. We found some gold, but not enough to be noteworthy for others.

When we got back, I told the owner of the American Ranch about the pass I had found, and he was excited. He had never dreamed of such a thing before.

Vocabulary:

imparted = made known, revealed

proprietor = owner

Francis Parkman: Trapper on the Oregon Trail

Shortly after Francis Parkman graduated from Harvard in 1844, he made plans to explore the West with friend and fellow Bostonian, Quincy Adams Shaw, and record his experiences for publication. The following excerpt from Parkman's journal of his trip in 1846 focuses on his observation of a trapper. The names mentioned in the text below refer to French Canadian trappers (Rouleau and Saraphin).

Summary:

The trapper Rouleau was gone for a limited time each year on his expeditions. The rest of the time he took it easy. When he was hunting he had to be very alert. Sometimes he ate uncooked food rather than attract Indians with a campfire. I met a trapper who had many scars from bullets and arrows, and who had broken an arm and shattered a knee. But, he kept on trapping.

Vocabulary:

lest = for fear that
mettle = courage, spirit
perilous = dangerous
privations = lack of basic
   necessities
rude = makeshift, crude
thither = in that direction

Like other trappers, Rouleau's life was one of contrast and variety. It was only at certain seasons, and for a limited time, that he was absent on his expeditions. For the rest of the year he would lounge about the fort, or encamp with his friends in its vicinity, hunting, or enjoying all the luxury of inaction; but when once in pursuit of the beaver, he was involved in extreme privations and perils. Hand and foot, eye and ear, must be always alert. Frequently he must content himself with devouring his evening meal uncooked, lest the light of his fire should attract the eyes of some wandering Indian; and sometimes having made his rude repast, he must leave his fire still blazing, and withdraw to a distance under cover of the darkness, that his disappointed enemy, drawn thither by the light, may find his victim gone, and be unable to trace his footsteps in the gloom. This is the life led by scores of men among the Rocky Mountains. I once met a trapper whose breast was marked with the scars of six bullets and arrows, one of his arms broken by a shot and one of his knees shattered; yet still, with the mettle of New England, whence he had come, he continued to follow his perilous calling.

Source: Francis Parkman, *The Journals of Francis Parkman.* First published in 1849, *The Oregon Trail* by Francis Parkman, NY: New American Library, 1950, pp. 185-7.

The Wagon Trains

by Katharine N. Emsden

Back in the overcrowded cities of the East, newspapers advertised the new lands of opportunity obtained by the Louisiana Purchase. Citizens over twenty-one who were willing to cultivate farmland for five years could claim 160 acres. The land race was on, and Oregon became the first destination. Lewis and Clark had shown the way across barren plains and mountain passes to the fertile Willamette Valley. For 200 years the wide Missouri River had separated the new European settlers from hundreds of tribes and trappers who travelled the paths according to the seasons.

Independence, Missouri was the town most often used as the point from which wagon trains were assembled and supplied for the overland trip to the West. Steamboat passengers poured into St. Louis and then headed for Independence to stock Conestoga wagons with enough provisions to last a year, and their personal belongings before disembarking. The wagons were pulled by teams of horses, mules, or oxen, and weighed up to 5,000 pounds, when loaded.

An early photo shows horse-drawn wagons along the trail. (Courtesy of the Denver Public Library, Western History Department)

Wagons from Independence followed the Santa Fe Trail for the first fifty miles and then were floated across the Kansas River before continuing along the north side of the Platte. During the spring run-off of the Rockies, the Platte River was often a mile wide, and yet it was always shallow enough to ford. The nearby path, created by buffalo and Indians, was the longest, easiest stretch of any overland trail. Mormons said it was "carved by the finger of God." Each diary describes the landmarks: Chimney Rock, Courthouse Rock, Scott's Bluff, and Independence Rock, where thousands were to scratch their names with a stone or buffalo bone.

The prairie was an eternity of space and changing skies. Weather played tricks. Phantom rain would pour in sheets that drifted toward earth and then suddenly evaporated. Static electricity could bounce off the horns of cattle and start a stampede. There was a dryness unknown in the East. Even the snow was drier here; it took 100 inches to melt into one inch of rain! Wooden wheels might shrink loose from their iron rims unless taken off and soaked overnight in the river to swell back to normal size. Thick lumps of oil oozed from the sand soil and provided lubrication for the axles when the train stopped for nooning. No one imagined the oil fields that lay beneath the trail.

For days the Rocky Mountains loomed up ahead, their dark silhouette concealing height and distance. Sweetwater Creek at the base of South Pass often necessitated attaching ropes on a pulley between trees on both sides. Women and children had to unload the wagons while the men swam with the oxen and then combined teams to stand on the far bank and pull the floating wagons over deep water. Herds of cattle followed, sometimes emerging far downstream. Often, during the first twenty years of migration, Sioux and Cheyenne from a nearby village came to help.

Pulleys, ropes, and chains guided the heavier wagons over steep crests, and a log or spare wagon tongue slowed the dangerous descent. It was not unusual for an entire load to tip over a narrow ledge and be lost forever. Early migrant families walked rather than ride in a wagon without brakes or springs.

Adequate water became the major problem after leaving the Rockies. Both boys and girls would help fill the barrels as they came upon a clear spring. In desperate thirst, livestock often headed for poisonous or alkali pools, and everyone rushed to drive them safely past. Cholera, yellow fever, or small-pox took lives on almost every large wagon train.

In 1850, '52 and '57, an almost unbroken line of 45,000 covered wagons rolled along the Oregon Trail each year from April to August, "like a great white serpent through a sea of green grass." A sort of prairie post office developed; strips of cloth or paper were pinned to trees, rocks, buffalo bones, and even human skulls! "Stewart Party took Sublette Cut-Off, June 10, 1853" "Water here is poison. We lost 6 of our cattle." In 1850, one sign on a Sierra pine tree read: "President Zachary Taylor has died." News was so scarce that some emigrants arrived at their destination without realizing that the area had just become the latest State in the Union.

The pioneers set off to tame the wilderness and start a new life. They gathered their families, cows, a hoe, and some seed bags, along with provisions for the first year, and departed from their past. Poet Gary H. Holthaus describes what it must have been like.

"West of the Missouri"
by Gary H. Holthaus

Fifty thousand persons in an endless
Train, says Hulbert,
Travelers and fellow travelers
Rarely out of sight
Of one another,
    "The ratio being 16 men to
    one woman and three women
    to every child."

And trudging with them
36,000 oxen, 18,000 horses,
7000 mules and milch cows,
And 2000 sheep,

All bent on crossing
My lively prairie,
Leaving scars
Like stretch marks on my belly,
Cutting a swath through buffalo
And elk, all the fair game;
Cutting me open at last
For gold or grain,
The people streaming
Into this new land,
Recreating the life
They thought they'd left behind.

Source: Gary H. Holthaus, *Circling Back*. Salt Lake City: Gibbs M. Smith, Inc., Peregrine Smith Books, 1984, "West of the Missouri," p. 73.

Summary:

An endless stream of 50,000 travelers were rarely out of sight of each other. There were 16 men to every woman and three women to every child. Thousands of oxen, horses, mules, milk cows and sheep went along with them. They were all determined to cross the plains, going through herds of buffalo and elk, to achieve their goals: sometimes, finding gold, other times, wanting to farm the land. They came to this new land, but they recreated the lives they thought they were leaving behind. (Note: The poet sees the prairie as a pregnant woman, with the wagon ruts being like the stretch marks that women get in late stages of pregnancy. Sometimes women have a baby by *Caesarean section*, when the doctor cuts her open to take the baby out. In this case, the prized baby could be gold or grain delivered from the land.)

Crossing the Plains in 1851

Harriet Talcott Buckingham was one of the many pioneers who kept her own account of the journey West. Following are excerpts from her journal written between May 4 and September 23, 1851.

Summary:

Summarize this journal in your own words.

May 4 Crossed the Missouri at Council Bluffs, where we had been a couple of weeks making the final preparations on this outskirt of civilization....

We number seven wagons—one carriage, a large band of oxen & cows, horses & mules—the latter are for the carriage—oxen for the wagons. Mrs Smith myself and a little girl occupy the carriage—we have a drive—Mr Smith rides a little black mule that is very intelligent & a pet with him.

There are drivers for the wagons and loose stock. Mr E. N. Cooke & family have a nice carriage & about the same equipment. Mr Hiram Smith has crossed the plains twice before & so knows how to do it Mr Smith & Cooke travel together intending to go by the way of Salt Lake City for the purpose of selling to the Mormons Goods & Groceries with which most of the wagons are loaded so we make quite a cavalcade as we slowly move along. We have tents & small cook stoves.

Mr & Mrs Smith have had the carriage so arranged that a bed can be made of the seats, & when the curtains are all buttoned down there is a comfitable sleeping apartment The little girl & I sleep in one of the big covered ox wagons in which is a nice bed—really makes a cosy little low roffed room, it has a double cover—Mr Smith has a coop fastened on behind the carriage which contains some fine white chickens—three hens and a rooster. We let them out evry time we camp, and already they seem to know when preparations are made for moving & will fly up to their place in the coop....

May 5 We are now travelling through the country of the Omaha Indians. They demand toll for passing so Mr Smith promises them a feast, & they have sent sumners [summoners?] out to bring in all the tribe who arc not already out Buffalo hunting

[May] 6 Hosts of the Indians have arrived on Indians Ponies. Squaws & little Pappooses— young men in the glory of fine feathrs paint & skins—their war costume, for they are just now about to go to fight the Pawnees. The girls who are in the market are most grotesqely painted in Vermillion & Green—they have not yet assumed the cast off garments of white people—The Calf which Mr Smith & Cooke gave them was killed and eaten even to the very entrails, some hard Bread was given to them too.

In the evening they gave us a war dance by an immense fire, that lit up the wiered [weird] hob goblin scene—their fiendish yells, as they tossed their arms about and swung the gory scalps just taken from their enemis, the Sioux: helped to give the whole affair an informal aspect.

11 May The Platte river is beutiful here— many islands dot the stream & are covered with cotton wood trees—We ladies went to visit some Indian Graves near here & were piloted by Mr Patton. Some of the graves were larger than others, all were mounds from five to six feet in highth. Earth & stones heaped up in a conical shape.

June 2 …At about noon we passed Ancient Bluff ruins…I climbed the highest ruin which commanded a fine view of the country. This is of Solid Rock with five scraggy gnarled cedars, Throwing their twisted arms over the over-hanging precapice Many a name was carved with knife upon the bark We left our names upon a Buffalo bone which lay bleaching upon the top….

Vocabulary:
conical = shaped like a
   cone
entrails = internal organs
grotesqely = grotesquely,
   distorted, bizarre
precapice = precipice,
   steep face of a cliff
Vermillion = bright red

23

Vocabulary:

Buffalo Chips = dried buffalo dung, used for making fires

chagrin = feeling of humiliation

consternation = amazement

correll = corral

countenances = facial expressions

specters = ghosts

June 5 …Camped upon the Platt our vision was delighted with the view of a few small trees that grew upon the banks for they tell strongly of good cheer after having to cook so long with Buffalo Chips For 200 miles we have no wood. Bluffs are not so high on the south—more sandy, rainy & unpleasant.…

[August] 15 Last night about midnight were awakened by the sudden tramping of the cattle who were herded in the correll. Indians! Stampede! before two moments elapsed all hands stood ready to fire—imagine to yourself forty men rising like specters from under waggons tents & carriages with guns & bowie knives—cattle, scattering with speed & the bright moon rising over our heads & then form a faint idea of the consternation & chagrin that momentarily depicted itself upon their countenances—when the guard said it was he who accidentally frightened them causing this small stampede...—Then all was quiet again.…

[August] 18 Travelled over sage plains, roads rocky and dusty Rocks sharp and hard. Bear River vally is the most inhabitable looking since we left the Platt The Crickets are large often an inch and a half or two inches in length Black & shiney, the Indians make soup of them —They catch them by driving them into pits dug for this purpose—they are dried for winter use,…our White Chickens try to swallow them, it often takes two or three efforts to get one disposed of, they are so numerous that one cannot avoid stepping on them.…

[August] 21 …Numbers of Shoshone Indians are camped here, We brought enough Salmon of them for a fish hook to make us wish never to see any more.

[September] 15 Crossed the Dechutes river —very rocky & difficult. We were told the story of an emigrant woman who was afraid to cross with her train, but was persuaded to get on a horse behind an Indian that had just crossed. When in the middle of the stream with dizzy brain she cried out in fear. The Indian turned his face to her & said, "Wicked woman put your trust in God" These words in good English frightened her worse then ever—

[September] 23 found us at the Dalles of the Columbia. Most of the train went on crossing the Cascades mountins & the rest of us came by boat & raft to the Portage of the Cascade, where we camped. The little steam boat James G Flint brought us part of the way...

Many fine canoes were to be seen, made of great length out of trunks of great cedar trees— some might be fifty feet in length hollowed out & carved with high sculptured prows, glistning with brass headed nails & it was wonderful to see the skill with which they would handle them. The squaws all seemed to be rich in ornaments of beads & brass strings of beads of all colors weighing pounds hang from the neck,—all looked happy and contented sevral Indian burial places we passed as we walked from one end of the portage to the other...

26 of sept we landed at Portland a little town of a couple hundred inhabitants, just as the guns were booming in honor of the completion of the Plank Road to Taulatin plains....

Source: H. T. Buckingham, "Crossing the Plains in 1851," *Covered Wagon Women: Diaries and Letters from the Western Trails, 1840-1890*, V. III 9 Vol. Kenneth L. Holmes, ed., Glendale, CA: The Arthur B. Clarke Company, 1989 [Document B].

Vocabulary:
prows = bow(s) of a ship

Devil's Gate

Devil's Gate, as painted by William Henry Jackson. (Denver Public Library, Western History Department)

John Hawkins Clark travelled on the Oregon-California Trail to Sacramento between May and September of 1852. Like others who kept daily journals, Clark described some of the key landmarks along the route.

Consider this:

When the pioneers and explorers travelled across the country, they used familiar natural landmarks to get their bearings. When people travel today, what kinds of landmarks do they use when getting directions to a certain place?

Vocabulary:

asunder = apart
discern = detect
perpendiculair=
   perpendicular, vertical

Clark's notes on seeing Devil's Gate

June 25 …The great rock lies just before us and we were eager to get upon its back…. The view from this elevation is a very extensive one….

Do you see yon huge range of mountains some four or five miles to the west? Well, do you see that it is split asunder from the bottom to the top, a narrow and perpendiculair opening of some 400 feet through solid granite rock? That little opening is called the "Devil's Gate." By looking very closely at the bottom of that opening you can discern a little silvery thread of water issuing from it…. I hardly know of a more interesting spot than that on the top of Rock Independence….

Source: John Hawkins Clark, *Overland to the Gold Fields in 1852*. Found in Kansas Historical Quarterly, XI, Louise Barry, ed., August, 1942, used with special permission of the Kansas State Historical Society.

Mormons Travel to Utah

Just as many of the early colonists had come to America to seek religious freedom, so did the Mormons migrate to the West to practice their faith without discrimination. Their leader, Brigham Young, kept a detailed journal of the Pioneer company of Mormons which headed from Winter Quarters, Nebraska to the Great Salt Lake in Utah, in 1847.

Brigham Young's Journal

April 23, 1847 – Friday. The Pioneer company started about noon, crossed Plum Creek and passed a large corn field, the corn stalks still standing, left Pawnee town, soon crossed Ashcreek twelve feet wide, one foot deep, and proceeded two miles to the place designated for crossing the Loup Fork river. A few attempted to cross with their wagons but owing to the quicksand bed of the river experienced difficulty.

Dr. Richards reported that he had rode through the Pawnee town about helf a mile west of us and had seen the ruins of about 175 houses or lodges averaging from twenty to sixty feet in diameter, all of which had been burnt to the ground by the Sioux Indians at a time when the Pawnees were absent on their hunting expedition.

The town had been partially fortified by an embankment of earth and sods about four feet high, having a ditch on the outside; this place has contained about six thousand souls who have been the terror of the Western tribes.

The Pioneer company met and after deliberation concluded to build two rafts about sixteen feet long each to carry over our goods on the morrow.

July 23, 1847 – Friday. The advance company moved about three miles and encamped; Elder Orson Pratt called the camp together, dedicated the land to the Lord, entreated the blessings on

Consider this:
Young notes much of what he sees with numeric descriptions. Why do you think this was important to him?

Vocabulary:
deliberation = discussion, debate
entreated = begged
on the morrow = tomorrow

Vocabulary:

ascended = went up

brethren = brothers

diligence = hard work

exhorted = urged with
strong argument

friable = readily crumbled

furrow = a narrow trench
made by a plow

harrow = a farm
instrument used to even
off plowed ground

Saints = Mormons were
referred to as saints by
other Mormons

tendered = offered

the seeds about to be planted and on the labors of His saints in the valley. The camp was organized for work. Elders W. Richards and Geo. A. Smith exhorted the brethren to diligence.

11:30 a.m., the committee appointed reported that 20 rods by 40 had been staked off by them on which to plant beans, corn, and buckwheet; soil friable, loam and gravel.

About noon, the first furrow was turned over by Wm. Carter. Three plows and one harrow were at work most of the afternoon.

At two p.m., a company started to build a dam and cut trenches to convey the water on to the land.

At three, thermometer 96 degrees. A company commencd mowing the grass and preparing a turnip patch.

At six, a thundershower passed over the camp. I ascended and crossed over the Big Mountain, when on its summit I directed Elder Woodruff, who had kindly tendered me the use of his carriage, to turn the same half way round so that I could have a view of a portion of Salt Lake valley.

The spirit of light rested upon me and hovered over the valley, and I felt that there the Saints would find protection and safety.

We descended and encamped at the foot of the Little Mountain.

Source: Brigham Young, 1847. Found on Heritage Gateway Site: http://heritage.uen.org/cgi-bin/websql/journalday

The Gold Rush

by Phyllis Raybin Emert

The gold and silver rushes of the middle to late 19th century changed the United States in a number of significant ways. When gold was discovered in 1848, the states of Missouri, Iowa, and Texas made up the western boundary of the country. Farther west lay an essentially uncivilized wilderness of regions and territories, populated by a variety of Indian tribes, immigrants, settlers, and exotic buffalo.

The discovery of gold, first in California, then in Colorado and Nevada, followed by major silver strikes in these areas, stimulated an extraordinary amount of economic growth. Efforts to meet the needs of the miners and other people who migrated to the West in droves led to unrivaled progress and expansion in agriculture, commerce, transportation, and industry.

As the population increased, so did the formation of towns, cities, and local government. The need for law and order evolved into an organized criminal justice system. This combination led to the eventual achievement of statehood, and, by the turn of the century, the continental United States was much as it is today, with the exceptions of Arizona and New Mexico (achieving statehood in 1912.)

Gold is Discovered at Sutter's Mill

In 1844, James Marshall left Missouri and headed to California to work for John Sutter near Sacramento. On January 24, 1848, while working at Sutter's Mill, Marshall saw something glittering in the American River. It was gold! Although Sutter and Marshall tried to keep it a secret, the news spread and soon "Gold fever" gripped the nation.

An eyewitness account

One morning Marshall discovered, much to his astonishment, some small shining particles in the sand at the bottom of the race, which upon examination he became satisfied were gold Of course, the news spread like wild fire, and in less than one week after the news reached Monterey, one thousand people were on their way to the gold region.... Every idler in the country, who could purchase, beg, or steal a horse, was off, and ere the first of August the principal towns were entirely descrted....

(continued on next page)

Vocabulary:

idler = someone who is idle, inactive

race = a channel which holds water in the mining process

29

Hundreds and sometimes even thousands of dollars were spoken of as the reward of a day's labour...and the mining population had swelled to about three thousand.... A few months after their discovery I saw men, in whom I placed the utmost confidence, who assured me that for days in succession they had dug from the bowels of the earth over five hundred dollars a day.

Source: E. Gould Buffum, *Six Months In The Gold Mines.* Edited by Caughey, The Ward Ritchie Press, 1959, originally published in 1850, pp. 50-2.

By 1849, there was a steady stream of eager gold seekers from the east heading to California. The migration lasted for years, and had a huge impact on the cities and towns along the way. Following are a newspaper article and a journal entry describing it.

Consider this:
Can you think of another time in history when so many people moved to another place? Describe the situation.

"the road is crowded…"

Hundreds of California and Oregon emigrants arrive in our city daily. From present appearances, the emigration will be larger than it was in 1849 or 1850. We learn by a gentleman who came through Hannibal [Missouri] by land, that the road is crowded with teams, and hundreds are daily crossing the Mississippi at various points. We notice among the emigrants several families, who go out with the intention of making permanent settlements.

Source: *The St. Joseph* [Missouri] *Gazette* - April 28, 1852. Found on http://www.stjosephmuseum.org

"it is a sight to see"

…I could not begin to tell you how many their [there] (are) in St. Joseph that are going to Oregon and California but thousands of them it is a sight to see the tents and wagons on the banks of the river and through the country they are as thick as camp meeting tents 20 or 30 miles and some say for 50 miles.…

Source: Mary Colby - 1852. Found on http://www. stjoseph-museum.org

Tools of the Trade
by Phyllis Raybin Emert

In the early days of the California gold rush, all a miner needed was a pickax, a pan, and a stream of water to be a prospector. This was referred to as placer mining. The water would clean the dirt from the stream-bed out of the pan, leaving the heavier gold flakes and nuggets at the bottom.

According to Robert Wallace in *The Miners*, "gold was unmistakable to anyone who had hefted it and clenched a bit of it between his teeth. Soft and malleable in its pure 24-carat form, gold was the only yellow metal that would not break when it was vigorously pounded or bent...."

The richest placers were found in foothill streams at the base of mountain ranges. Gold was likely to collect in ridges and holes of stream-beds or in gravel, sand, or clay banks which were often located in the bends of a river.

After gold was discovered in Colorado, Nevada, Montana, and the Dakotas between 1859 and 1876, more sophisticated techniques and equipment came into use. Instead of pans, miners used rockers, then Long Toms to increase production. Others sank holes directly into the bed-rock to find the richer deposits of gold. Some dammed up streams and rivers, and constructed separate waterways called races. They built wooden flumes to carry water to sites where the earth needed washing. The following excerpts, written by eyewitnesses, describe some of the processes and equipment used by miners.

...The apparatus...which has always been the favourite assistant of the gold-digger, was the common rocker or cradle.... It consists of...a wooden box or hollowed log, two sides and one end of which are closed, while the other end is left open. At the end which is closed and called the 'mouth' of the machine, a sieve, usually made of a plate of sheet iron, ...perforated with holes about half an inch in diameter, is rested upon the sides. A number of 'bars' or 'rifflers' which are little pieces of board from one to two inches in height, are nailed to the bottom, and extend laterally across it. Of these [the] ...one at the 'tail,' ...is...where the dirt is washed out. This with a pair of rockers like those of a child's cradle, and a handle to rock it with, complete the description of the machine....

Source: E. Gould Buffum, *Six Months In The Gold Mines.* Edited by Caughey, The Ward Ritchie Press, 1959, originally published in 1850, pp. 36-8.

Consider this:
For many of the gold seekers, the mining equipment and methods were all new. Can you think of anything comparable today?

Vocabulary:
apparatus = equipment
hefted = lifted, carried
laterally = side to side
malleable = pliable

Black and white prospectors worked the "Long Tom."

Consider this:

Choose a task that you do often, and describe it in detail to someone who doesn't know how to do it and has never seen any of the equipment which might be used in performing the task. (Examples might be mowing the lawn, delivering newspapers, doing the laundry, etc.)

Vocabulary

cullender = colander

perforated = punched with rows of holes

slat = a narrow strip of metal or wood

trough = a long, narrow receptacle

"The Long Tom"

...In many places the surface-soil, or in mining phrase, the 'top dirt,' 'pays' when worked in a 'Long Tom.' This machine...is a trough, generally about twenty feet in length, and eight inches in depth, formed of wood, with the exception of six feet at one end, called the 'riddle,' ...which is made of sheet iron, perforated with holes about the size of a large marble. Underneath this cullender-like portion of the 'long-tom,' is placed another trough, about ten feet long, the sides six inches perhaps in height, which divided through the middle by a slender slat, is called the 'riffle-box.' It takes several persons to manage, properly, a 'long-tom.' Three or four men station themselves with spades, at the head of the machine, while at the foot of it, stands an individual armed 'wid de shovel and de hoe.' The spadesmen throw in large quantities of the precious dirt, which is washing down to the 'riddle' by a stream of water leading into the 'long-tom' through wooden gutters or 'sluices.' When the soil reaches the 'riddle,' it is kept constantly in motion by the man with the hoe. Of course, by this means, all the dirt and gold escapes through the perforations into the 'riffle-box' below, one compartment of which is placed just beyond the 'riddle.' Most of the dirt washes over the sides of the 'riffle-box,' but the gold being so astonishly heavy remains safely at the bottom of it.

Source: Louise Clappe, ed., *The Shirley Letters from the California Mines*. New York: Alfred A. Knopf, 1949, originally published in 1854-55, pp. 132-36.

"where to find the gold"

Because there have been so many misrepresentations of this gold region, I shall attempt to describe it faithfully. Gold is found just about where the mountains begin; there is nothing in the valley. The mountains are almost perpendicular, and a mountain a mile or more in height is a frequent sight. Nearer to the river there are rocks which are sometimes fifty yards high, all more or less steep, and often perpendicular. In the cracks of these volcanic mountains the gold gravel is found. It has been washed down from the mountains by heavy rainstorms. Wherever these rocks do not exist, there is no gold. The gold hunter must creep around among these rocks and has to scrape the gold gravel with a hatchet or a shovel. Then he pours it into his sack and carries it to the river. He has to be very careful to jump from one rock to another in just the right way, otherwise he might easily break his legs or his neck. When he has carried his sack up to the river, one hundred to two hundred and fifty feet away, he must wash the gravel....

(continued on next page)

Consider this:
Why do you think the author wanted to describe the search for gold more accurately?

Explain several factors that would have caused the gold prospectors to misrepresent the process and the outcome.

Panning for gold, by Jeff Pollock, based on a water-color painting by O.C. Seltzer. (Thomas Gilcrease Institute, Tulsa, Oklahoma)

Vocabulary:

yoke = a crossbar designed to be carried across the shoulders to hold equal loads suspended from each end

Now the question arises, how much can a man earn by this dirty and exhausting work? When I arrived at the river, everything had been dug up and the best part of the gold was already gone....

...everyone was busy with wheel-barrow, shovel and hoe, digging into the gold-containing earth. Everyone carries two pails on his shoulder, suspended from a yoke. The yoke, pails and soil together weigh a hundred and twenty-five pounds. This burden is carried for two hundred and sixty-five paces up to the river. In order to spare myself the weight of the yoke and the pails, I filled a sack with the soil and carried it to the river where my younger son daily washed about two hundred and fifty pailfuls. This quantity was worth from twelve to fifteen dollars....

Source: H. B. Scharmann, *Scharmann's Overland Journey To California.* Translated by Zimmermann and Zimmermann, Freeport, NY: Books for Libraries Press, 1969, originally published in 1918, pp. 55-7, 73.

Women in the Mining Towns

Although few women participated in the early days of the gold and silver rushes, their numbers increased considerably with time. According to Robert Wallace in *The Miners*, "Women were so scarce in the mining frontier that any female was treated with a respect that sometimes verged on idolatry." A San Francisco census of 1847 listed 138 women among 459 residents. By the end of 1853, there were around 8,000 in that city.

Women found that they could earn money in several ways. Miners were willing to pay well for a good meal, clean clothes, and to sleep in a clean bed. As a result, many women made small fortunes by running boarding houses.

Luzena sets up a hotel

I determined to set up a rival hotel. So I bought two boards from a precious pile belonging to a man who was building the second wooded house in town. With my own hands I chopped stakes, drove them into the ground, and set up my table. I bought provisions at a neighboring store, and when my husband came back at night he found, mid the weird light of the pine torches, twenty miners eating at my table. Each man as he rose put a dollar in my hand and said I might count him as a permanent customer. I called my hotel 'El Dorado.'

Source: Luzena Stanley Wilson, Nevada City, 1850. Found in Joann Levy, *They Saw The Elephant*, Hamden, CT: Archon Books, 1990, p.114.

Summary:

I was determined to set up a hotel. I bought wood and made a table. I bought provisions, and when my husband came home, he saw 20 miners eating at my table. They each paid $1.

Vocabulary:
El Dorado = a legendary place in South America where gold and precious metals could be found
precious = costly

Dance halls were popular with the miners. (Library of Congress)

The Pony Express

To the pioneers who survived their journeys west, whatever their reasons for going, there was great relief in finally being able to settle down after the 2,000 mile journey. But, it didn't take long before they felt cut off from their loved ones at home. In the mid 1800s, letters from New York to California took 30 days by steamship around South America, while the overland mail took at least 23 days for delivery.

William H. Russell, William Bradford Waddell and Alexander Majors, who worked in the freight business, proposed a faster mail service between St. Joseph, Missouri and Sacramento, California by a Pony Express with letters to be delivered in just ten days. They made their plans in January and February of 1860, and by April of that year the system was in place. Up to 80 young riders were hired at the rate of $100 to $125 per month. Station keepers, stock tenders, route superintendents, and horses also needed to be found.

Stations were located from 5 to 20 miles apart, and here the riders would get on fresh horses and go about 75 miles a day. There was great hope for this venture, and local politicians and journalists followed it closely. The Pony Express only ran for 19 months, and never did make any money for its founders, but it was quite an astounding achievement in America's communications history. It was a only matter of time before the telegraph and the transcontinental railroad would be replacing the Pony Express, across the nation.

Summary:

It's a great day for the city of St. Joseph, for 10 years the gateway to the West.

Now it will be the connecting point for both coasts, and mail will be delivered overland.

Some day trains will bring passengers from St. Joseph to California in less than a week.

Vocabulary:

portal = gateway
prophetic = predicting the
    future

Major M. Jeff Thompson's prophetic speech on the first day of the Pony Express

"This is a great day in the history of St. Joseph [Missouri]. For more than a decade she has been the portal through which passed the wagon trains for the great west.

"Now she is to become the connecting link between the extremes of the continents. For the first time in the history of America, mail will go by an overland route from east to west.

"The time will come when steam will drive a railroad train through those fastness' and bear passengers from St. Joseph to California in less than a week.

"I see you smile, my fellow citizens, and nudge each other at the idea I am harboring. Some of you are saying, 'Jeff is dreaming as usual of the impossible and unknown,' but I tell you all that, as sure as I stand here, the day will come when at this very town you may board a train which will take you through the gold fields, and that within a very few years.

"More than that, I say to you the wilderness which lies between us will blossom as the rose, cities will spring into existence where the Indians and Buffalo now hold possession. Mountains will be tunneled, streams bridged and the iron monster which has become mankind's slave will ply between our confines and those far distant shores.

"As the Indian vanishes, the white man takes his place. Commercial activities will replace the teepee and the campfire. Schools and colleges will spring into existence and the refinements of civilization will span the continent.

"Of all these things, the California Overland Express is the forerunner. Hardly will the cloud of dust which envelopes the galloping pony subside before the puff of steam will be seen upon the horizon.

"Citizens of St. Joseph, I bid you three cheers for the Pony Express — three cheers for the first overland passage of the United States Mail."

Source: Major M. Jeff Thompson, found on website: http://www.xphomestation.com/frm-stories.html

(Courtesy of the Library of Congress)

Summary:
Some of you think I'm only dreaming, but I'm sure some day you'll be able to board a train here and go all the way to the gold fields.

The wilderness will blossom into cities, where now there are Indians and buffaloes. Trains will have tunneled through mountains and bridged streams, taking us to distant shores.

When the Indian disappears, the white man will take his place. Businesses will replace campfires and tepees, and schools and colleges will be built.

The Overland Express is just the beginning; the railroads will take over.

Citizens of St. Joseph, I congratulate you for the Pony Express.

Consider this:
Left is an artist's rendering of a Pony Express rider greeting the men installing telegraph poles and wires. How would the telegraph lead to the end of the Pony Express?

Summary:

Summarize this article in your own words.

Vocabulary:

dispatches = a written message sent with speed

The New Overland Express Company

The San Francisco TELEGRAM, of March 15th, has the following particulars of this enterprise:

...Fifty horses have already been purchased towards the road on this side. The animals will be immediately placed at the stations to be selected along the route, and the first express mail will leave this city on Monday, April 3d, at 4 o'clock P.M., and is to leave here each Monday there after. The express will leave here by boat for Sacramento; at that point it will take horse, and be transported on horseback to St. Joseph, Mo.

At 6 o'clock P.M., of the day after leaving this city, the express will receive dispatches at Carson City, by telegraph; these dispatches will be delivered to the telegraph operator at St. Joseph, and from there transmitted to their destination. The schedule time between Carson City and St. Joseph is nine days. So a dispatch sent by telegraph from San Francisco to New York, on the evening of the 4th of April, will be delivered in the latter city on the morning of the 13th, and an answer will be received here on the 22nd.

A letter sent from here by express on the 3d will be delivered in New York on the 15th, and the answer can be received here on the 29th. The Company expect to be able to carry from thirty to fifty pounds of express matter. Their stations will be from twenty to twenty-five miles apart, and as great care has been exercised in the selection of animals... and the choice of riders, there is no doubt but the Company can make the time inside of the schedule.

The charges on matter, we learn, will be $3 per half-ounce from this city to Salt Lake, and $5 per half-ounce for all points beyond that....

Source: Found on website: http://www.xphome station. com/frm-stories.html

The Transcontinental Railroad

President Lincoln signed the Pacific Railroad Act on July, 1 1862, and one of the greatest adventures in American history began.

Two railroad companies, the Union Pacific and the Central Pacific, were authorized to construct a railroad and telegraph line that would span a continent. The Union Pacific was to build westward from the 100th meridian (near Omaha, Nebraska) across the Great Plains, and the Central Pacific was to build eastward from Sacramento through the Sierra Nevadas.

In addition to the land grants, the government promised funds to each of the railroads depending on how much track was laid, touching off a fierce competition between the two. Soon the silent lands that had been the providence of nomadic Native Americans, fur traders, and explorers gave way to the bustle of surveyors, graders, trestle builders, tunnel blasters, and spikers. Thousands of workers, including Civil War veterans and immigrants, were enlisted to do the back-breaking work of laying track across the treeless deserts and through towering granite mountains. As the tracks from the Central Pacific and Union Pacific approached each other, the two railroads could not agree on a meeting point; as a result, they surveyed and graded a parallel roadbed.... Finally, they chose a meeting point—Promontory, Utah—and on May 10, 1869, a telegraph key clattered out a message indicating the line's completion.

Source: Bureau of Land Management, Environmental Education Homepage: http://www. blm.gov/education/railroads/steam.html

Rails Across the Continent
by Jeanne Munn Bracken

Men had been thinking of a railroad across the American continent for years, but as the 1860s dawned, the nation was mired in the Civil War. The war was to some extent both good news and bad news for the dreamers. The Civil War showed once and for all how important railroads were for moving soldiers and supplies quickly from one hot spot to another.... On the other hand, the four-year war consumed manpower, financial resources, and the attention of the policymakers in Washington.

The Central Pacific broke ground in Sacramento on January 8, 1863, to the amusement of bystanders. The Union Pacific broke ground on December 8, 1863, and never laid another foot of track for a full year....

All the expected difficulties arose—and more. Indians attacked surveying crews, which often worked well ahead of the track builders; they also tore up survey stakes and caused accidents by blocking the tracks. The huge buffalo herds that thundered across the plains were another problem; they damaged tracks and knocked down telegraph poles, which they discovered made fine scratching posts during molting season.

Weather was another enemy of the railroad construction crews. Bitter snowy winters halted most construction in the Sierra Nevadas. Spring thaws in the mountains and on the plains turned streams and dry gulches into raging torrents that washed out tracks and trestles. Thunderstorms, wind, drought, avalanche, dust storms—all these tormented the railroads. And still they built.

The Central Pacific didn't have much trouble with the Native Americans; they allowed them to ride free whenever they wanted. By the spring of 1869, they had laid 690 miles of track over, around, and through the Sierra Nevadas into Utah. The Union Pacific, building over easier terrain, covered 1095 miles of plains, foothills, and Rocky Mountain passes into Utah.

The two lines met at Promontory Summit, Utah, on May 10, 1869. The continent was conquered.

Source: Jeanne Munn Bracken, ed., *Iron Horses Across America: The Transcontinental Railroad.* Carlisle, MA: Discovery Enterprises, Ltd., 1995, pp. 8-12.

The men build the railroads and the railroads build the towns

As the railroads were being built, it became clear that the exact location of tracks and stations would have a tremendous impact upon the people living nearby. If the tracks bypassed a certain town, even by a few miles, then the town became isolated, almost immediately. If, on the other hand, a station was built where no town had existed before, the economy suddenly boomed, creating great wealth and opportunity. Below, Frithjof Meidell, an immigrant worker from Norway, described the situation in a letter to his family.

Summary:

The railroads are building up the whole country. Farmers get wider markets and can get higher prices. Even the old apple woman runs to the train to sell apples to the passengers.

"...railroads put new life into everything..."

Dear Mother:

...[You asked] How is the railroad getting along? Here in America it is the railroads that build up the whole country. Because of them the farmers get wider markets and higher prices for their products. They seem to put new life into everything. Even the old apple woman sets off at a dogtrot when she hears that whistle to sell her apples to the passengers. Every ten miles along the railways there are stations, which soon grow up into towns. "Soon," did I say? I should have said "immediately," because it is really remarkable how rapidly the stations are transformed into little towns. I can but compare it with the building of Aladdin's castle by means of his wonderful lamp, only that things move still faster here, where it is not necessary to sit and rub a rusty old oil lantern. Here you can buy houses all ready to be placed on the freight car, and in half a day's time they can be nailed together.

...I shall attempt to describe how these towns spring up. First—that is, after the two old log houses that stand one on each side of the tracks —first, I say, the railroad company builds a depot. Next, a speculator buys the surrounding 100 acres and lays it out in lots, streets, and a marketplace. Then he graces the prospective town with the name of an early President or a famous general—or his own name—holds an auction, and realizes many hundred percent on his investment.

A young wagonmaker who has just completed his apprenticeship hears about the station, that it is beautifully located in a rich farming country, is blessed with good water, and, most important of all, that it has no wagonmaker. Making a hasty decision, he buys the barest necessities for setting up in his profession, hurries off to the place, rents one of the old log houses, and is soon at work. One absolute necessity he still lacks, however: a sign, of course, which is the most important part of a man's equipment here in America. The next day he hears that there is a tramp painter aboard the train; he gets him off, puts him to work, and the very next day the farmers are surprised to see a monstrous sign straddling the roof of the old log house.

continued on next page

Summary:
The stations are transformed into little towns very quickly. You can buy ready-made houses, which arrive by train and can be nailed together in half a day.

I'll describe how it happens. The railroad company builds a train depot, and then an investor buys land near it. He lays out lots, streets and a shopping area. Then he names the town.

A young wagon-maker hears about the good farmland and the natural resources, and learns that there is no wagon-maker in the area. He sets up a business there. But he needs one more thing —a sign. When he learns of a tramp painter aboard an incoming train, he convinces him to stay and paint signs. The next day, the farmers see the huge sign hanging on the log house.

Men's clothing shop in Cripple Creek, Colorado. Note store and hotel signs.

Summary:

The sign works well, and local farmers start to place orders from the wagon-maker. But the work is more than he can handle. So, he writes to three newspapers, and soon hires apprentices to help him.

When another train comes along, a blacksmith gets off, and rents the other log house. He makes a lot of noise hammering, and soon everyone knows there's a blacksmith in town.

Within a week, a carpenter, a tailor and a shoemaker come to town.

The sign is an immediate success, for the farmers rush to the shop and order wagons, wheels, and the like. The poor man is overwhelmed with more work than he can handle for ever so long. He is about to regret that sign notion of his, but suddenly he has another idea. He accepts every order, and no sooner are the customers away than he seizes his pen and writes to the editors of three different newspapers that three good apprentices can secure steady work with high wages in the "flourishing town of L." Within two days he has help enough, and the work goes "like a song."

The train stops again, and off steps a blacksmith who went broke in one of the larger towns. …Off he goes and rents the other log house and nails a horseshoe over the door as a sign. The horseshoe to be sure, cannot be seen at any great distance, but the smith has a remedy for this, and he starts to hammer and pound away at his anvil so that the farmers for miles around can hear the echoes. They immediately flock to his door, and there is work enough for the blacksmith.

Within a short week, a carpenter, a tailor, and a shoemaker also arrive in town. The wagoner orders a house from the carpenter and rents the second story to the tailor and the shoemaker.

Soon the blacksmith also builds a house, and things progress with giant strides toward the bigger and better.

Again the train stops. This time two young fellows jump off, look around, and go over to have a chat with the blacksmith. One of them is a doctor, the other a lawyer. Both of them rent rooms from the blacksmith and start business.

Once more the locomotive stops. [A German man gets off]…he looks about inquiringly as if searching for something and steps up to the doctor to ask if there is a restaurant in town. On receiving a negative reply, his face brightens again; and after a short conversation with the doctor and lawyer, he steams off with the next train and jumps off at the first big town, where he…buys a barrel of whiskey, another barrel of biscuits, two large cheeses, tobacco, cigars, and sausages—miles of them. Thereupon he engages a painter to make an appropriate sign, and in three days he is back again in the new town. Now he rents the blacksmith's old log house and rigs it up as a shop. Soon the sign swings over the door, the whiskey barrel is half empty, and the sausages are dispatched by the yard.… His best customers are the railroad workers, most of whom are Irishmen.… The German, the blacksmith, and the tailor do a rushing business.…

Within a few years the town is very large. The wagonmaker owns practically half of it. The German deals only in wholesale. The lawyer is mayor of the town, and the blacksmith does nothing but smoke cigars, for now he is a man of affluence.

Source: Frithjof Meidell, 1855, *Archives of America*, vol. 8, pp. 349-53. Found in Jeanne Munn Bracken, ed., *Iron Horses Across America: The Transcontinental Railroad*, Carlisle, MA: Discovery Enterprises, Ltd., 1995.

Summary:

Things progress rapidly: the blacksmith builds a house, the others start their own businesses.

Then a doctor and a lawyer come to town. They too start businesses.

Then a German traveler arrives. He asks the doctor if there is a restaurant in town. When he finds out that there is none, he stocks up on food and supplies and opens one. His best customers are the Irish railroad workers. All do well in their businesses.

Within a few years, the town is thriving. The wagon-maker owns almost half of the town. The German only sells wholesale. The lawyer becomes the mayor of the town, and the black-smith doesn't work— he just smokes cigars, because now he is very rich.

Vocabulary:
affluence = wealth

The Irish and the Chinese

The biggest problem facing both the Central Pacific and Union Pacific Railroads was finding workers. Two groups of immigrants, the Irish and the Chinese, as different from each other as night and day, filled the gap. Charles Crocker, one of the owners of the Central Pacific, gave the Chinese a chance.

Summary:

I remember that I had a lot of trouble trying to get Mr. Strobridge to try Chinese workers. I remember that one pay day some Irish workers wanted to get a pay increase. I told Mr. Strobridge to get Chinese workers instead, and the Irish men begged us not to, and went back to work. A few months later, he did hire about 50 Chinese. Then he continued to hire more of them, until we had about ten or twelve thousand.

Vocabulary:

recollect = remember

The Chinese

"I recollect that I had a great deal of trouble to get Mr. Strobridge (the construction leader) to try Chinamen. At first I recollect that four or five of the Irishmen on pay day got to talking together and I said to Mr. Strobridge there is some little trouble ahead. When I saw this trouble impending, a committee came to us to ask for an increase of wages. I told Mr. Strobridge then to go over to Auburn and get some Chinamen and put them to work. The result was the Irishmen begged us not to have any Chinamen come, and they resumed their work. It was four or five months after that before I could get Mr. Strobridge to take Chinamen. Finally he took in fifty Chinamen, and a while after that he took in fifty more. Then, they did so well that he took fifty more, and he got more and more until finally we got all we could use, until at one time I think we had ten or twelve thousand."

E.B. Crocker, Charles' brother, wrote a letter in 1865 regarding the Chinese.

Summary:

A large part of our workforce is Chinese. They get almost as much work done as the white workers, and are much more reliable. They wouldn't think of striking. We train them to do all kinds of work.

"…A large part of our force are Chinese and they prove nearly equal to white men in the amount of labor they perform, and are far more reliable. No danger of strikes among them. We are training them to all kinds of labor, blasting, driving horses, handling rock, as well as the pick and shovel."

Source: Lynn Rhodes Mayer and Kenneth E. Vose, eds., *Makin' Tracks: The Story of the Transcontinental Railroad in the pictures and words of the men who where there.* New York: Praeger Publishers, Inc., 1975, p. 28.

The Irish

Where the Central Pacific solved its labor problem by hiring the Chinese, the Union Pacific turned to ex-soldiers from the Civil War, freed slaves, and especially to the wave of Irish immigrants who came to America to escape the potato famine in Ireland. Although they were good workers, the Irish had a reputation of being rowdy trouble-makers in their leisure time.

The Irish working on the railroads were also known as tarriers. Their job in later years was to stand beside the steam drills and move the loose rock. This well-known folksong was written by a tarrier named Thomas Casey.

Drill, Ye Tarriers, Drill

Ev'ry morning at seven o'clock
There was twenty tarriers a-working at the rock,
And the boss comes along, and he says kape still,
And come down heavy on the cast iron drill,
And drill, ye tarriers, drill!

>*Chorus*
>Drill, ye tarriers, drill!
>It's work all day for sugar in your tay;
>Down behind of the railway,
>And drill, ye tarriers, drill,
>And blast! and fire!

The boss was a fine man down to the ground,
And he married a lady six feet round.
She baked good bread and she baked it well,
But she baked it hard as the holes in hell,
And drill, ye tarriers, drill!

The new foreman was Jean McCann,
By God, he was a blame mean man.
Last week a premature blast went off,
And a mile in the air went big Jim Goff,
And drill, ye tarriers, drill!

When the next pay day came round,
Jim Goff a dollar short was found.
When he asked, "What for?" came this reply,
"You're docked for the time you was up in the sky."
And drill, ye tarriers, drill!

Source: *Fireside Book of Folk Songs*, by Margaret Bradford Boni. New York, Simon and Schuster, 1947, pp. 138-9.

Summary:
   Summarize this song
in your own words.

Vocabulary:
docked = had pay
   withheld
kape = keep
premature = earlier than
   expected
tay = tea

Loans, Grants, Scandals and Hearings

The Pacific Railway Act gave each company loans from the Treasury of $16,000 for each mile of track laid in the flat plains, $32,000 for each mile of track laid in the Great Basin, and $48,000 for each mile of track laid in the mountains. It also provided for each company to receive 10 sections (6,400 acres) of public land grants, mineral rights excluded, on each side of the track for each mile of track built. In 1864 a second Pacific Railway Act was passed increasing the land grants for each company to 20 sections per mile. In total, the companies received 33 million free acres of land. The…Act also gave the companies rights to the iron and coal deposits on the land grants and moved the federal loans to second-mortgage status so that the Union Pacific and Central Pacific could issue first-mortgage bonds for sale to private investors.

…[Theodore D.] Judah had formulated plans for the Central Pacific project, [and then] it was necessary to enlist men of means who could finance and carry on the building of the railroad. …four men who finally took hold of the enterprise had been obtained…Leland Stanford, Collis P. Huntington, Mark Hopkins, and Charles Crocker…known as "The Big Four."

Source: By Rebecca Cooper Winter, found on website: http://cprr.org/Museum/Eastward.html

Credit Mobilier

The Credit Mobilier was a construction company that helped build the Union Pacific Railroad. The company was owned by some Union Pacific stockholders who gave the construction company huge contracts. They were funneling money from Union Pacific…into Credit Mobilier, where they owned a majority of the stock. With Union Pacific receiving government subsidies and funds, the investors were stealing government money. To avoid a governmental inquiry into the transaction, the investors gave Credit Mobilier stock to members of Congress. A congressional investigation in 1872 revealed many congressmen, high ranking republicans, and vice-president Schuyler Colfax took stock in the company.

The…scandal during President Ulysses S. Grant's administration lead to a congressional inquiry that included the following testimony taken from Collis Potter Huntington of the Central Pacific Railroad so that the practices of the two railroads could be compared by the committee.

Source: Found on website: http://www.ripon.edu/academics/pogo/presidency/Grant/Scandals.html

REPORT OF THE SELECT COMMITTEE OF THE HOUSE OF REPRESENTATIVES, APPOINTED UNDER THE RESOLUTION OF JANUARY 6, 1873…

Q. Who composed the first board of directors ?
A. Governor Stanford, Charles Crocker, Theodore D. Judah, Charles Marsh, Phil. Stanford, Mark Hopkins, and myself.…

. . . .

Q. After the organization of the company what means were resorted to for the construction of the road ?
A. We commenced to build the road on our own means. We got some aid from the Government which we thought would let us through the mountains; but soon gold began to rise, (and we paid for everything in gold,) and we saw that we were going to have great difficulty. In fact, I made up my mind that we were not going to get through with the Government bonds and first-mortgage bonds. We then went to the State legislature, and the legislature agreed to pay the interest for twenty years on a million and a half of bonds. Gold kept rising, and we saw that we were still going to have difficulties. Our engineer's estimate was $88,000 a mile for getting across. Iron was $40 a ton when the estimate was made, and it went up to about $140. The expense of going around the Horn and taking the war-risks was so great that freights went up very high, and we cast about again, putting in our own money all the time, which was considerable. About that time the city of San Francisco voted to give us $600,000, or to take our stock to the amount of $600,000 and to give us $600,000, of their 7 per cent bonds. Afterward the work looked so heavy that they did not like to take the stock, believing it was of no value.

(continued on next page)

Summary:

Q: who made up the first board of directors?

A: He names them.

Q: After the company was organized, how was the road (railroad) to be built?

A: We started to build on our own and then we got some government aid. We thought we'd have enough money, but as gold began to rise in value, we had trouble. I decided we wouldn't use government bonds. So we went to the state legislature and they agreed to pay the interest for 20 years on 1.5 million dollars. But gold kept rising and we still had trouble paying. The engineer estimated that it would cost $88,000 per mile to build the road. When we made the estimate, iron was only $40 per ton; now it is $140. When we had to get supplies delivered around Cape horn, it was very expensive because of the war, so we kept putting in more of our own money. About that time San Francisco was going to give us $600,000 in exchange for stock, but they weren't sure our stock was worth it.

Summary:
We finally compromised and the city gave us $400,000 and did not take our stock. They thought they had made $200,000 on the deal. That, I believe answers your question.

Q: I find fraud and illegal activity here for the materials and work which were really done by the directors of your company to benefit themselves. You were making payments to your own contracting company for an amount of over $225 million. Do you know of any dividends made to your company around that time?

A: No.... I don't know where they got those figures.

We finally compromised with San Francisco, and the city gave us $400,000 and did not take the stock, and they considered they had made $200,000 by the operation, so that we got $400,000 out of the city as a donation.... That I believe answers the question as to how we got our means to build the road.

. . . .

Q. I find...fraudulent and illegal pretense of paying for the said materials, work, &c., which really in fact had been furnished and done by the said directors and confederates for their own benefit, the said last-mentioned directors and confederates from time to time voted to pay and deliver, and make over in the name of the Central Pacific Railroad Company to the said Contract and Finance Company and its confederates, large sums of money, and large amounts of bonds, lands, and other valuable assets of the said Central Pacific Railroad Company of great value, to wit, of the value of $225,855,618.17. Now, do you know of any dividends made to the Contract and Finance Company at or about the period of November 6, 1867?

A. No; I do not. I do not know where they got those figures....

Source: Collis P. Huntington and Congressional Committee, Washington: Government Printing Office. 1873. Found at website: http://www.ripon.edu/academics/pogo/presidency/Grant/Scandals.html

Promontory Point
by Jeanne Munn Bracken

No point had been fixed for the Central Pacific and the Union Pacific tracks to meet. Originally the Central Pacific was supposed to cross the Sierra Nevada Mountains and stop, but the Railroad Act of 1864 allowed them to keep going. Since they received government grant money for each mile of road they completed, each company was eager to get as large a portion as possible.

The final months of construction became a contest to see which railroad could get the farthest in the fastest time. This competition culminated in a legendary day, April 29, 1869, when the Central Pacific crews laid ten miles and fifty-six feet of track in one twelve-hour day. As the end neared, the companies sabotaged each other's work.

It took a Joint Resolution of Congress to set the final meeting point at Promontory Summit, Utah—fifty-six miles west of Ogden and bypassing Brigham Young's Mormon community at Salt Lake City to the south.

A ceremony marking the union was held at Promontory on May 10, 1869, two days behind schedule. The trainload of Central Pacific dignitaries had been delayed by an accident in the Sierras and the Union Pacific bigwigs by a washout at the Devil's Gate Bridge in Wyoming. The joining was symbolized by the driving of four special spikes (only one of them gold).

One was inscribed "May God continue the unity of our country as this Railroad unites the two great Oceans of the world." Lofty expectations indeed for rival companies who had been warring only days before! Leland Stanford of the Central Pacific and Thomas Durant of the Union Pacific each took a mighty swing to drive the ceremonial spike. Both missed, to the amusement of the construction crews standing by.

The race had captured the imagination of Americans on both coasts much as the space race did a century later—but without modern communication methods. Those were the days of newspapers and, at the end, it was the newfangled telegraph, whose lines marched across prairie and mountain pass with the tracks, that carried the message: Done! The continent was bound by iron rails.

The completion of the transcontinental railroad was only the beginning of the race to reach every part of the continent by rail. From central points in the country, tracks reached like fingers grasping for new towns and cities.

Based on a painting of the joining of the Union and Pacific railroads.

Research Activities/Things to Do

- Lewis and Clark led a team called the "Corps of Discovery" on their 28-month expedition to explore the West. These men had special skills needed to survive in the wilderness. In what ways do you think their selection and training were similar and dissimilar to that of our modern day astronauts?

- On pages 6-9 are excerpts from Thomas Jefferson's instructions to Lewis and Clark. What were his main interests in their expedition?

- Pike's Peak in Colorado was named for Zebulon Pike, who attempted to cross that snow-covered mountain in the early 1800s. How many other geographic locations can you think of which were named after prominent people in American history? What about in your own community?

- Investigate the large fur trade markets of St. Louis, Missouri and Taos, New Mexico during the first half of the 19th century. Why are they no longer major export markets?

- What traces did the pioneers leave as they traveled and why? (discarded baggage, graves, writings, etc.)

- What impact did a wagon train have on the environment?

- What was the impact of the pioneers' experience on their language—what new words evolved as a result of their journey? What effect did contact with peoples of different backgrounds (Native Americans, Mexicans, etc.) have on their language? (Source: Activities from http://heritage.uen.org/cgi-bin/websql/classroom.hts)

- Dayton Duncan, in "From Out West" (Source: *Travels in the Americas.* NY: Newcombe, Weidenfeld & Nicholson, 1989, p. 62) said: "Prejudices are like heavy furniture in a Conestoga wagon on the Oregon Trail. In order to keep moving forward, sometimes you have to toss them out, even if they are family heirlooms." Discuss what Duncan means by this.

- What might have happened differently in the settling of the West that would have preserved Indian culture, the buffalo, etc.?

- List some of the reasons for the migration of European settlers to the West in the mid-to-late 19th century.

- Based on your readings, create your own journal of your trip West, in the mid-to-late nineteenth century, assuming the role of wife, cook, etc. Choose one of the trails marked below, and learn enough about the geography to make the journal realistic.

- Settlers risked their lives traveling west, in search of spiritual freedom, economic opportunity, adventure. What would it take for you, personally, to pull up stakes and move to another place, far away from where you now live, assuming that you will probably never again see your family and friends—except those that accompany you on your journey? Plan to leave most of your possessions behind, too!

- Francis Parkman kept a detailed travel log of his explorations in the West. Keep a journal of the next trip you take, either local or afar, keeping in mind that a future generation might read it to learn more about life in the early 21st century based on your detailed observations.

- Many of the pioneers who went west kept detailed journals of their trips. The Mormons, the 49'ers, families traveling on wagon trains, and others kept fascinating accounts of their daily experiences, which is why we know so much about this period in history. Discuss whether or not these first-hand accounts have a different feeling to them than the kind of newspaper and television reports we see and hear today.

- Equipment for mining became more sophisticated as the number of miners increased. Technologies for separating the gold and silver improved. Can you think of another situation in which technology and production progressed rapidly to meet the demands of a new market? Explain.

- Research the growth of cities like Sacramento and San Francisco as result of the gold rush.

- In the early days of the gold and silver rushes, law and order was easily maintained. Crime was almost nonexistent, as everyone felt he had an equal chance to succeed in becoming rich. Only when some became wealthy and others poor, did crime increase. How does this relate, or does it, to the crime rate today?

- In plotting the course of the railroads through the central and western parts of the nation, whole cities could be made or destroyed. Explain.

- Most history text books focus on the roles of men in the gold and silver rushes. How did women contribute to and benefit from the growth of western towns directly resulting from the search for riches?

- Mail order brides traveled from the East to marry prospectors and merchants in the dominantly male towns and cities in the West. Compare this practice to that of responding to "personal ads" found in today's newspapers and on the internet.

- James P. Beckwourth, a trapper and scout, and York, William Clark's slave, were black Americans who helped to explore the West. Both were thought to be Indians by some of the western tribes who had never seen black men before. Why do you think we don't know much about them or about other blacks who helped to build the West?

- Research other blacks who participated in the westward expansion of the 1800s, with special focus on the blacks who migrated west after the Civil War.

- Why does history show us so little about the Mexicans, Blacks, and Native Americans who played significant roles in the development of the West? Consider who was recording the events and why.

- Do your own research on the key developers of the transcontinental railroad and document some of the corruption and political influences.

- At first, the developers thought that the Chinese might be too small and frail to work on the building of the railroads. They were proven wrong. Research the part that the Chinese played in constructing the railroads in America.

- When labor was scarce during the Civil War, signs reading "No Irish Need Apply" were taken down. Indeed, the Irish contributed greatly to building the nation's railroads. How else did prejudice play a role in developing a labor force for the construction of the transcontinental railroad?

- After considering the San Francisco newspaper announcement below, think about how the railroads put a swift end to the Pony Express.

NOTICE.

BY ORDERS FROM THE EAST,

THE PONY EXPRESS

WILL be DISCONTINUED.

The Last Pony coming this way left At-
chison, Kansas, yesterday.
oc25-1t   WELLS, FARGO & CO., Agents.

- If you could have been a participant in the exploration, development and settling of the West, would you prefer to have participated in the Lewis and Clark expedition, the fur trade, the gold rush, the Pony Express, or the building of the railroads? Explain your choice.

Sample Photo

- Pictured above is a photo of the interior of a loaded Conestoga wagon. Describe what you can about the family who might have traveled West in it. Include comments about their economic status, family size, genders of occupants, etc.

- Based on the items contained in the wagon, create a story or a page from a journal about a character who traveled in this wagon.

- Assume that this wagon with all of its contents was taken by an Indian tribe in exchange for horses. Which of its contents would have been unfamiliar to the Indians in the early days of the Oregon Trail? (Late 1840s)

- Anaylze the above photo using the worksheet on the following page.

Analyzing Photos Worksheet

Some or all of the following will help you to analyze an historic photo, or other type of graphic. Use the worksheet to jot down notes about the piece being evaluated.

1. **What is the subject matter?**

2. **What details provide clues?**
    - ❑ scene
    - ❑ clothing
    - ❑ style of graphic
    - ❑ B&W/color
    - ❑ buildings
    - ❑ artifacts
    - ❑ written message
    - ❑ people
    - ❑ time of day
    - ❑ season

3. **Can you determine the location?**   **The intended audience?**

4. **What is the date? If there is no date, can you guess the period?**

5. **What is the purpose of the photo, etc.?**
    - ❑ private use
    - ❑ art
    - ❑ recording an event
    - ❑ advertising
    - ❑ propaganda
    - ❑ Other_____

6. **Can you tell anything about the point of view of the graphic?**
    - ❑ social
    - ❑ recreational
    - ❑ political
    - ❑ sales tool
    - ❑ educational

7. **What details make this piece effective or ineffective?**

8. **What can you learn about the people who lived at this time from the photo?**

9. **Are any symbols used in the graphic? Are they verbal or visual? Describe what each symbol represents.**

    <u>Object</u>   <u>Symbolizes</u>

Suggested Further Reading

The books listed below are suggested readings in American literature, which tie in with the *Researching American History Series*. The selections were made based on feedback from teachers and librarians currently using them in interdisciplinary classes for students in grades 5 to 12. Of course there are many other historical novels that would be appropriate to tie in with the titles in this series.

Exploring the West and Pioneers on the Trails West
The Cabin Faced West, Jean Fritz - EL
The Oregon Trail, Francis Parkman - HS
Prairie Songs, by Pam Conrad - M
Call Me Francis Tucket, Gary Paulsen - EL/M
Roughing It, Mark Twain - M/HS
Dear Levi: Letters from the Overland Trail, Elvira Woodruff - M
High Trail to Danger, Joan Lowry Nixon - EL
Weasel, Cynthia De Falise - M
The Journal of Joshua Loper, A Black Cowboy, Walter Dean Myers - EL
Voices from the West: Life Along the Trail, Katharine N. Emsden, ed. - M/HS
   (nonfiction)
Westward Expansion: Exploration and Settlement, Cheryl Edwards, ed. - M/HS
   (nonfiction)

The Gold and Silver Rushes
Augusta Tabor: A Pioneering Woman, Betty Moynihan - M/HS
The Journey of Wong Ming-Chung, A Chinese Miner, Laurence Yep - EL
By the Great Horn Spoon, Sid Fleischman - M
All That Glitters: The Men and Women of the Gold and Silver Rushes,
   Phyllis Raybin Emert, ed. - M/HS (nonfiction)

The Transcontinental Railroad
Dragon's Gate, Laurence Yep - M
The Great Railroad Race,The Diary of Libby West, Kristiana Gregory - EL
A Family Apart, Joan Lowry Nixon - EL/M
Train Song, by Diane Siebert - EL
Iron Horses across America: The Transcontinental Railroad, Jeanne Munn
   Bracken, ed. - M/HS (nonfiction)

For information on these and other titles from Discovery Enterprises, Ltd., call or write to: Discovery Enterprises, Ltd., 31 Laurelwood Drive, Carlisle, MA 01741 Phone: 978-287-5401 Fax: 978-287-5402